KN

A New True Book

KENYA

By Karen Jacobsen

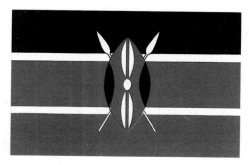

Flag of Kenya

CHILDRENS PRESS®
CHICAGO

A dancer of Kenya's
Samburu tribe

PHOTO CREDITS

Bettmann/Hulton—28, 37 (left)

© Cameramann International, Ltd.—8 (top & bottom left)

Candee Productions—© John Ketcham, 37

© Virginia R. Grimes—12 (right), 13, 15 (left), 20

Reprinted with permission of *The New Book of Knowledge*, 1989 edition, © Grolier Inc.—4

Historical Pictures Service, Chicago—27 (2 photos)

© Jason Lauré—34, 37 (bottom right), 41 (left), 42

Nawrocki Stock Photo—© Leslie C. Street, 17 (left)

Odyssey/Frerck/Chicago—© Robert Frerck, 9, 17 (right), 22 (left), 38 (top left & top right), 39, 40 (right), 43

Photri—18; © L. Astrom, 38 (bottom left); © Dr. Joe Atchinson, 45 (bottom)

© Ann Purcell—Cover Inset

R/C Photo Agency—© Earl L. Kubis, 12 (left)

Root Resources—© Dave G. Houser, 45 (top)

© James P. Rowan—19

© Bob & Ira Spring—4, 25, 30, 40 (left), 44 (top)

Stock Imagery—© Charles G. Summers, Jr., 15 (right)

SuperStock International, Inc.—8 (right), 11; © Hubertus Kanus, Cover; © Walter Shostal, 22 (right); © I.A. Mehar, 38 (bottom right); © Giorgio Ricatto, 41 (right)

TSW/CLICK-Chicago—© Dave Saunders, 2; © Peter Carmichael, 7 (left); © James P. Rowan, 44 (bottom)

UPI/Bettmann Newsphotos—33 (2 photos)

Valan—© V. Wilkinson, 7 (right)

Cover—Nairobi

Cover Inset—Kilaguni Tsavo

Library of Congress Cataloging-in-Publication Data

Jacobsen, Karen.
  Kenya / by Karen Jacobsen.
    p.   cm. — (A New true book)
  Includes index.
  Summary: Introduces Kenya, home to more than forty
African tribes as well as people from Asia and Europe.
  ISBN 0-516-01112-X
  1. Kenya—Juvenile literature. [1. Kenya.]
I. Title.
DT433.522.J33 1991   90-20009
967.62—dc20   CIP
                                            AC

TABLE OF CONTENTS

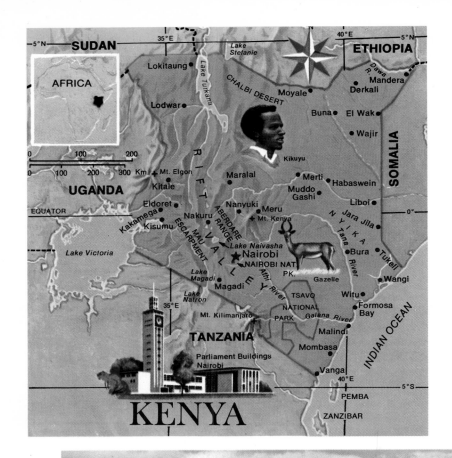

Zebras stop to drink in Tsavo National Park.

THE NATION

Kenya is a nation on the east coast of Africa.

The equator passes through the middle of Kenya. Much of the country is very hot, but in the west the land is high and cool.

Kenya shares borders with five countries—Tanzania, Uganda, Sudan, Ethiopia, and Somalia. The Indian Ocean forms Kenya's eastern border.

Lake Nyanza—also known as Lake Victoria—is the largest lake in Africa and forms part of Kenya's western border. Lake Turkana, also called Lake Rudolf, lies in northern Kenya.

The Republic of Kenya is the home of more than twenty-five million people. It is a democracy. Voters elect a president and the members of a National Assembly. The National Assembly makes Kenya's laws.

A farm worker (left) picks coffee beans.
Sisal plants (right) grow in warm climates.

Farming is the most important economic activity in Kenya. In the highlands, farmers raise coffee, corn, tea, sugarcane, wheat, and sisal. (Sisal is used to make rope and rugs.)

7

Nairobi (above) is a large, modern city. Kimathi Street (above left) is in downtown Nairobi. The Parliament building (left) houses the National Assembly.

Kenya's capital and largest city is Nairobi. Almost one million people live in Nairobi.

There are no valuable minerals in Kenya. It has very few industries. There are some food-processing factories and textile plants.

Kenya has no oil, but there is an oil refinery at Mombasa.

An oil refinery in Mombasa. Gasoline, heating oil, and other petroleum products are made here.

THE LAND

Kenya has three major land regions—the coastal lowlands along the Indian Ocean, the inland plains, and the southwestern highlands.

In the coastal lowlands, the land is flat. In the southern part of the coastal lowlands, the soil is good for farming. The weather along the coast is hot and humid with plenty of rainfall. The

The port city of Mombasa. The Galana River is at the top right.

city of Mombasa, Kenya's
main seaport, lies at the
mouth of the Galana River.
The flat, dry inland
plains region spreads over
three-quarters of Kenya.
Thornbushes and dry

11

grasses cover much of the area. Small groups of nomads live on the inland plains. In the north, the Chalbi Desert lies near the Ethiopian border.

The southwestern region of Kenya is called the

A "dust devil" (left) whirls along the hot, dry inland plains of Kenya. Snow-capped Mount Kenya (right) rises in the center of the country. At 17,058 feet, it is the highest point in Kenya.

Farmlands under cultivation near Nairobi

highlands. It is a hilly, green land with rich soil and plenty of rain.

Kenya's best farmland is in the highlands. More than 80 percent of Kenya's people live and work in the highlands.

In Tsavo National Park, tourists can get close to some of the park's thousands of elephants.

NATIONAL PARKS

In Kenya large sections of land have been set aside as national parks. Wild animals roam free in the parks.

Nairobi National Park covers 44 square miles near Nairobi. Tsavo National Park on the Galana River, Kenya's

Water holes in Tsavo National Park (left) attract many kinds of wildlife. Lions (right) are among the many big cats that make their home in Kenya.

largest park, covers more than 8,000 square miles. Aberdare National Park is in the highlands.

Wild animals such as elephants and lions are protected. Kenya's parks attract thousands of tourists from around the world.

15

THE PEOPLE OF KENYA

More than seventy different languages are spoken in Kenya. But Swahili and English are the official languages.

Swahili is an ancient African language. *Safari* is a Swahili word meaning "journey." *Uhuru* means "freedom." And *harambee* means "pulling together." *Safari*, *uhuru*, and

These people are Kikuyu. With a population of about two million, the Kikuyu are Kenya's largest tribe.

harambee are all very important words in the Republic of Kenya.

Kenya is home to about 40 African tribes. The largest tribe is the Kikuyu. One out of every five Kenyans is a Kikuyu. Other tribes are the

A Luo elder, in ceremonial dress

Luo, the Luhya, the Kalenjin, and the Masai.

The Kikuyu, who live in the highlands near Mount Kenya, are very good farmers. Many Kikuyu are college graduates and work as government leaders, doctors, lawyers,

In a Kikuyu farming village, the houses have grass roofs and walls made of sticks and mud.

and business people. Many live and work in Nairobi.

The Luo people also farm land in western Kenya. Many Luo are fishermen on Lake Nyanza. Other Luo are skilled mechanics who work in shops and factories.

The Luo and the Kikuyu are ancient rivals. Sometimes the two tribes fight. They compete for land and power in Kenya.

The Masai people live in southwestern Kenya. Their villages are called *kraals*.

A group of Masai warriors. One man is wearing a magnificent lion's-mane headdress.

The Masai keep large
herds of cattle and goats.
They are nomads. They
move from place to place to
find grass for their animals.

Trading ships from Arabia
have sailed south to the
coast of Kenya for more than
a thousand years. Some of
the traders built trading
posts and married into the
Swahili tribe.

The Arab-Swahilis grew
very rich and powerful.
Today, there are several

The Arab-Swahilis follow the Islamic faith. This boy (left) attends an Islamic school in Lamu, Kenya. Many Asians, such as these Indians in Nairobi (right), own shops in Kenya's cities.

thousand Arab-Swahilis living along the coast of Kenya.

People from many European countries— Portugal, Germany, Great

Britain, and others—have come to live in eastern Africa. In the late 1800s, the British took power and made Kenya into a British colony.

Today, there are fewer than 40,000 European Kenyans. Most are business people and their families. There are fewer than 60,000 Asian Kenyans. Most are Indians whose ancestors came from India in the 1890s to build the Nairobi railroad. Today, the Asians live in Kenya's cities.

LONG AGO IN KENYA

About three thousand years ago, tribes from western Africa came to Kenya. They were hunters and food gatherers. Later settlers were herders and farmers.

In the A.D. 500s, Arab ships sailed along the eastern coast of Africa. By the 900s, the Arabs had trading posts at Mombasa and on the island of Lamu off the coast of Kenya.

THE PORTUGUESE

Portuguese traders built this fort at Mombasa in 1593.

In 1498, a ship from Portugal sailed around the Cape of Good Hope and into the Indian Ocean.

Later, in the 1500s, more Portuguese arrived. They built their own trading centers. In time, the Portuguese took control of all trade on the eastern coast of Africa. But in the 1700s, the Arabs returned and took back their trading empire.

25

WHITE EXPLORERS

In the early 1800s, people from several European countries explored Africa. They wanted to find its treasures and take control of the land.

Johann Ludwig Krapf and Johannes Rebmann were German missionaries. In the 1840s, they explored the inland region of eastern Africa.

British explorers John Hanning Speke (left) and Richard F. Burton (right) traveled into the interior of Kenya in search of the source of the Nile River.

In the 1850s, two British explorers, John Hanning Speke and Richard F. Burton, tried to find where the Nile River began. Speke was the first European to reach Lake Nyanza and show how it was linked to the Nile.

27

Henry Stanley (left) finds Dr. Livingstone. Stanley later crossed central Africa from east to west.

Henry Stanley went to Africa in 1869 to find Dr. David Livingstone, a missionary who was missing somewhere in Africa. Stanley found Livingstone, wrote about the adventure, and became famous.

GREAT BRITAIN IN KENYA

By 1895, Great Britain had taken control of Kenya. They called it British East Africa. The British took the best land in the highlands from the Kikuyu and other tribes. They set up large farms and hired Africans to do the work.

In 1920, the western part of British East Africa became Kenya Colony. It was a paradise for white people. But Africans were

A Kikuyu tribal chief and his wife

not welcome, except to work as servants and laborers.

Many Africans wanted to get their lands back. They wanted the whites and the Asians to leave.

In 1944, the Kikuyu and some other tribes formed the Kenya African Union (KAU). The KAU tried to find legal ways to change the laws that kept black Africans from voting.

In 1946, after the end of World War II (1939-1945), about five million black people and only thirty thousand white Europeans lived in Kenya.

The white Kenyans wanted independence from Britain. They wanted their white government to rule Kenya. But the blacks wanted *uhuru*. They wanted to form their own black government.

JOMO KENYATTA

In 1947, Jomo Kenyatta, a Kikuyu, became the leader of the KAU. As a child, Kenyatta had been a student in a mission school. Later, he went to school in England.

Other black people in Kenya formed terrorist groups called *Mau Mau*. The Mau Mau attacked and killed whites and blacks— and anyone else who stood in their way.

By 1952, the British army and the Mau Mau were at war.

In 1952, police rounded up over two thousand Africans (left) for questioning.
They were looking for members of the Mau Mau. Other Kikuyu warriors (right)
were trained to fight the Mau Mau.

The British arrested Kenyatta
as the leader of the Mau Mau.
In 1953, he was sent to jail
for nine years.

When the war ended in
1956, more than 13,000 blacks
and about 130 Europeans
and Asians had been killed.

UHURU AND HARAMBEE

On December 12, 1963,
Kenya became independent
from Great Britain. The black
voters elected Jomo Kenyatta
president of the new nation.

Kenyatta's government
passed some important new
laws. The government

divided many of the large, white-owned farms into smaller farms, which were sold to black Kenyans.

Kenyatta believed in *harambee*. He tried to get all of Kenya's people—the black tribes, the Asians, and the Europeans—to work together and stop being enemies. But many Asians and Europeans feared the black government, and left the country. Many black tribes feared the power of the Kikuyu.

PROBLEMS

When Jomo Kenyatta died
in 1978, many people thought
there would be trouble. But
there was peace. Vice-president
Daniel T. arap Moi, a Kalenjin,
was elected president. Moi
continued many of Kenyatta's
programs.

Today, Kenya has many
serious problems. Every year
there are many more people.
There are shortages of food,
housing, and jobs. The water
supply is not clean, and there

President Daniel T. arap Moi (left) must deal with
Kenya's poverty. Shantytowns surround the city of
Nairobi (top). People go to "food shacks" (right) to get food.

is much disease in the country.
The government is trying
to create more jobs. It is
training Kenyans to produce

37

A Kikuyu girl from the highlands (top left). Members of the Masai tribe (bottom left). A Kikuyu worker picking tea (top right). A textile worker in a Nairobi spinning mill (bottom right).

more food and to improve health care. Also, the government is trying to keep peace among its people.

EDUCATION

Many adults in Kenya cannot read or write because they had no schools to go to when they were young. But most of today's children get at least an elementary school education.

An elementary schoolteacher in Nairobi

In Kenya, the first four years of primary school are free. But there are fees for the next three years and for high school.

More than 80 percent of Kenya's children attend schools. Most of the schools are in towns and cities. The classrooms are crowded and books must be shared. Some children live in remote areas and cannot go to school.

At the University of Nairobi, students earn degrees in medicine, law, engineering, and other advanced subjects. Kenya also has colleges for training students in agriculture, teaching, health care, business, and other skills.

People of all Kenya's tribes and races are represented at a graduation ceremony (left) at the University of Nairobi (right).

Schools and clubs throughout Kenya have soccer teams.

SPORTS AND RECREATION

The favorite sport in
Kenya is football (soccer).
Most Kenyans are fans of
their national soccer team.
Many of Kenya's finest
athletes are long-distance
runners. They have set

This Olympic poster by Mr. Soi honors
Kenya's remarkable long-distance runners.

speed records in the
Olympic Games and other
international sports contests.

Kenya is a young and
proud nation. Its people
have many differences and

43

Chania Falls (above) is one of the loveliest of Kenya's many waterfalls. Lush palm trees (below) grow near Kenya's coast.

many problems. But they are working together—practicing *harambee*—to improve their lives in their beautiful land.

WORDS YOU SHOULD KNOW

ancestor (AN • sess • ter)—a grandparent or relation earlier in history

colony (KAHL • uh • nee)—a settlement of people from another country

degree (dih • GREE)—a rank or title given by a college or university to a person whose work has fulfilled certain requirements

democracy (deh • MAHK • rah • see)—a government in which the people vote and pick the people they want to run their government

economic activity (ek • ih • NAH • mik ak • TIHV • ih • tee)—the things that people do to earn a living, such as farming or working in a factory

equator (ih • KWAY • ter)—an imaginary line around the earth, equally distant from the North and South poles

harambee (ha • RAHM • bee)—a Swahili word that means "pulling together"

humid (HYOO • mid)—damp, moist

independence (in • dih • PEN • dince)—freedom from the control of another country or person

minerals (MIH • ner • ilz)—useful substances such as oil, iron ore, or diamonds that are found in the ground

missionary (MISH • un • air • ee)—a person sent to a foreign country by a religious organization to spread its faith or to help the people there

nomads (NO • madz)—people who move from place to place to find a food supply or pasture for their animals

refinery (rih • FYNE • er • ee)—a place where oil is made into gasoline and other petroleum products

remote (rih • MOHT)—far away; far from settled areas

rivals (RYE • vilz)—people who compete for the same things

seaport (SEE • port) — a city or town built on the seacoast that has places for ships to load and unload cargoes

shortage (SHOR • tij) — a lack; too small an amount, as a shortage of food

terrorist (TAIR • er • ist) — a person who uses violence or threats to gain political ends

textile (TEX • tyle) — cloth

tourist (TOO • rist) — a person who visits a country on vacation

uhuru (oo • HOO • roo) — a Swahili word meaning "freedom"

INDEX

About the Author

Karen Jacobsen is a graduate of the University of Connecticut and Syracuse University. She has been a teacher and is a writer. She likes to find out about interesting subjects and then write about them.